STECK-VAUGHN
Elements of Reading

Comprehension

Scott G. Paris, Ph.D.

Interactive Meaning Builder

Science

Teaching Version

Harcourt Achieve

Rigby · Steck-Vaughn

www.HarcourtAchieve.com

1.800.531.5015

Level B

Acknowledgments

Supervising Editor	Erin Kinard
Senior Editor	Terra Tarango
Editor	Victoria Davis
Associate Director of Design	Cynthia Ellis
Senior Design Manager	Alexandra Corona
Associate Director of Production	Mychael Ferris-Pacheco
Production Coordinator	Paula Schumann
Editorial Development	Jump Start Press
Production Services	Lehigh Digital

ISBN 0-7398-9070-0

Printed in China

2 3 4 5 6 7 8 9 10 985 08 07

Teaching Version

Explicit, differentiated instruction: what you need, when you need it!

What the Teaching Version Has	What This Means for You
● Explicit instruction at point of use	● You can provide great instruction with very little planning.
● Quick and easy format	● You can deliver targeted instruction at the right moment, without interrupting the flow of reading.
● Differentiated instruction for English Language Learners	● You can tailor instruction to individual needs to ensure success for all.
● Instruction based on the extensive, research-proven work of Scott Paris	● You can be sure the instruction you provide is grounded in research and proven in the classroom!

How to Use this Teaching Version

1. Direct children to the appropriate lesson in their Interactive Meaning Builders.

2. Have the class read the selection at the same pace—either as a teacher read-aloud; a choral reading; or a silent reading, specifying ahead of time where to stop on each page.

3. Use the targeted instruction in the margins to develop children's understanding and use of strategies.

Introduce the comprehension focus with explicit instruction in key skills and strategies.

During reading of the selection, pause at the number icons to provide the corresponding instruction.

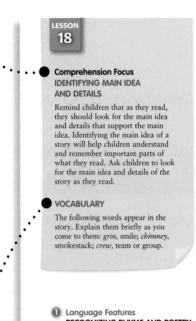

LESSON 18

Comprehension Focus
IDENTIFYING MAIN IDEA AND DETAILS

Remind children that as they read, they should look for the main idea and details that support the main idea. Identifying the main idea of a story will help children understand and remember important parts of what they read. Ask children to look for the main idea and details of the story as they read.

VOCABULARY

The following words appear in the story. Explain them briefly as you come to them: *grin*, smile; *chimney*, smokestack; *crew*, team or group.

① Language Features
RECOGNIZING RHYME AND POETRY

■ Rhyming words have the same sound at the end. Let's read the first two sentences aloud and listen for rhyming words. What rhyming words did you hear? *(own and alone)*

■ This story has rhyming words and a special beat or rhythm. What kind of story is it? *(a poem)*

6 Lesson 18

LESSON 18

THE HOUSE THAT JACK'S FRIENDS BUILT

Young Jack didn't have a house of his own.
He wanted to build one, but couldn't alone. ①
So he called on his friends and said with a grin,
"Will you help build my house? It's time to begin." ②

Why did Jack call on his friends?
○ He was sad.
○ He needed a ride somewhere.
● He needed help building his house.

6

② Explicit Meaning
UNDERSTANDING TEXT AND IMAGES

■ Read aloud the last two lines on this page. Then look at the picture of Jack's friends holding tools. What are Jack and his friends getting ready to do? *(They are going to build a house.)*

Use these definitions to help children understand difficult or important words.

Use the explicit instruction and interactive questions to deepen children's comprehension.

Use the sample answers to check children's responses to interactive questions.

Clear labels identify each prompt according to the comprehension building block and specific skill it addresses.

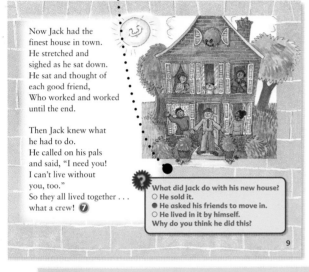

Now Jack had the finest house in town. He stretched and sighed as he sat down. He sat and thought of each good friend, Who worked and worked until the end.

Then Jack knew what he had to do. He called on his pals and said, "I need you! I can't live without you, too." So they all lived together . . . what a crew! **7**

? What did Jack do with his new house?
○ He sold it.
● He asked his friends to move in.
○ He lived in it by himself.
Why do you think he did this?

9

7 Explicit Meaning
UNDERSTANDING TEXT

■ Think about how Jack's friends helped him build a house. Why did Jack ask his friends to move into the house when it was done? *(They worked well together and he missed them.)*

ENGLISH LANGUAGE LEARNERS

Write a label for each part of the house that Jack and his friends built, including *walls, floor, chimney,* and *roof*. Model how to say each word and match it to the correct part of the illustration in the story. Have children repeat the names and then point to that part of the house in the story.

● **Finishing Up**
MODEL IDENTIFYING MAIN IDEA AND DETAILS

Create a main idea chart to help children review the main idea and supporting details in the story.

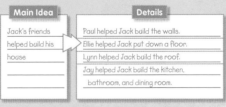

Main Idea	Details
Jack's friends helped build his house	Paul helped Jack build the walls.
	Ellie helped Jack put down a floor.
	Lynn helped Jack build the roof.
	Jay helped Jack build the kitchen.
	bathroom, and dining room.

The House That Jack's Friends Built   9

Guide the class through the "Finishing Up" Activity to model the comprehension focus of the lesson.

Help English Language Learners access the text by developing related oral language.

Comprehension Building Blocks

The point-of-use instruction is strategic and purposeful. It addresses the building blocks children must understand in order to fully comprehend any given text.

Text Features—*titles, headings and captions; highlighted, boldfaced, and underlined text; photos, illustrations, maps, graphs, and charts.*

Language Features—*unfamiliar and important vocabulary words, proper nouns, repeated words, and words related to the main ideas in the text; language that is used for alliteration, rhyme, imagery, and humor.*

Explicit Meaning—*the literal meaning of words, sentences, and images.*

Implicit Meaning—*drawing conclusions or making inferences about the text and images.*

Conceptual Meaning— *understanding the themes and concepts in the text as well as understanding the overall meaning of the selection.*

Interactive
Meaning Builder

Science

Level B

Comprehension

Interactive
Meaning Builder

Science

This book belongs to

_____

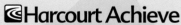

Rigby · Steck-Vaughn

www.HarcourtAchieve.com
1.800.531.5015

T5

Acknowledgments

Supervising Editor	Erin Kinard
Senior Editor	Terra Tarango
Editor	Victoria Davis
Associate Director of Design	Cynthia Ellis
Senior Design Manager	Alexandra Corona
Media Researchers	Nicole Mlakar, Stephanie Morris
Associate Director of Production	Mychael Ferris-Pacheco
Production Coordinators	Paula Schumann, Ted Krause
Technical Coordinator	Alan Klemp, David Hanshaw
Production Specialists	John-Paxton Gremillion, Greg Gaspard, Donna Cunningham
Image Trafficking	Joyce Gonzalez

Illustrations

Tom Barrett: pp. 66, 67, 68, 68, 69, 70, 71; Laura Bryant: pp. 6, 7, 8, 9; Patrick Gnan: pp. 5, 18; Patrick Merrell: pp. 19, 20, 21; XNR Productions: pp. 57, 58, 59, 60, 61. Elizabeth Wolf: p. 35; Jason Wolf: pp. 30, 31, 32, 33.

Photo Acknowledgments (Photo credits below are for the student book and accompanying electronic version.)

Cover ©Kevin Schafer; toc (Nessie sculpture) ©Hulton Archive/Getty Images; p.2 (tadpole) ©G.I. Bernard/Photo Researchers, Inc.; p.3 (toad) ©Linda Richardson/CORBIS; p.4 (poison sack) ©Animals Animals; p.5 (frog) ©Rod Planck/Photo Researchers, Inc.; p.10 (dart frog) ©James P. Rowan/DRK Photo; p.10 (ant) ©Barry Runk/Stand/Grant Heilman Photography; p.10 (ladybug) ©Oscar Poss/Taxi/ Getty Images; p.11 (bee) ©Zefa/Masterfile; p.11 (wasp) ©Bill Beatty; p.12 (coral snake) ©Mitsuhiko Imamori/Minden Pictures; p.12 (milk snake) ©Patricia Fogden/CORBIS; p.13 (monarch) ©Pete Turner/The Image Bank/Getty Images; p.13 (Viceroy) ©Mark Cassino/SuperStock; p.15 (sailfish) ©Norbert Wu/Peter Arnold, Inc.; p.16 (hummingbird) ©Russell C. Hansen/Peter Arnold, Inc.; p.16 (dwarf goby) Courtesy of Royal Canadian Museum; p.17 (Goliath spider) ©Wernher Krutin/PhotoVault; p.18 (T-Rex) ©Ira Block/National Geographic Image Collection; p.19 ©Black Hills Institute of Geological Research, Inc.; p.20 (skull) ©Ira Block/National Geographic Image Collection; p.20 (teeth) ©DK Images; p.22 (bats flying) ©Stephen Kraseman/Getty Images; p.24 (Short-tailed fruit bat) ©Stephen Dalton/Animals Animals; p.25 (Greater-horseshoe bat) ©Stephen Dalton/Animals Animals; p.26 (Loch Ness monster) ©Hulton Archive/Getty Images; p.27 (newspapers) Courtesy Solo Syndication Ltd.; p.28 (Loch Ness monster) ©David Greenwood/Getty Images; p.28 (Nessie sculpture) ©Hulton Archive/Getty Images; p.29 (submarine) ©Hulton Archive/Getty Images; p.36 (volcano) ©Timothy Shonnard/Getty Images; p.39 ©Larry Prosor/SuperStock; p.41 (volcano) ©Stephen & Donna O' Meera/Photo Researchers, Inc.; p.41 (Catskills) ©Francis X. Driscoll; p.42 (Great Rift) ©Jim Tuten Earth Scenes/Animals Animals; p.44 (computer) ©David Young-Wolff/Photo Edit, Inc.; p.45 (chipmunk) ©Tom & Pat Leeson/DRK PHOTO; p.49 ©Bob Krist/CORBIS; p.50 (Julia's tree) © Shaun Walker Otter Media; p.51 (Julia Hill) © Shaun Walker Otter Media; p.53 (treehouse hotel) ©Paul Rocheleau Photography; p.54 (ice hotel) Courtesy of Louis DeCharme; p.55 (underwater hotel) Courtesy of Jules Undersea Lodge; p.56 (picnic) ©Frozen Images/The Image Works; p.63 (walrus) ©Brian & Cherry Alexander; p.64 (Inuit children) ©Paul A. Souders/ CORBIS; p.64 (Sami woman) ©Brian & Cherry Alexander; p.65 (Arctic winter) ©Richard Elliott/Tony Stone Images/ Getty Images; p.65 (Arctic summer) ©Charles Mauzy/CORBIS.

Additional photography by Artville/Getty Royalty Free; BrandX/Getty Royalty Free; DigitalVision/Getty Royalty Free; EyeWire/Getty Royalty Free; ImageState Royalty Free; Photos.com Royalty Free; Photodisc/Getty Royalty Free; PhotoSpin Royalty Free; Royalty-Free/CORBIS and StockByte Royalty Free.

ISBN 0-7398-9063-8

Hello!

This book is full of fun stories for you to read. There are questions you can answer along the way. Answering these questions will help you understand and remember the stories!

Happy Reading!

Contents

Amazing Animals

Animals: Fact and Fiction

Our Planet Earth

Climates of Our World

Comprehension Focus
COMPARING AND CONTRASTING

Tell children that an article can compare by telling how things are alike. It can contrast by telling how things are different. Tell children that as they read, they should be thinking about how frogs and toads are alike and different.

VOCABULARY

The following words appear in the article. Explain them briefly as you come to them: *tadpole,* a baby frog or toad; *webbed,* having skin between the toes; *poison,* something harmful to touch or taste.

LESSON

1

Frogs and Toads ①

Tadpole

2

What is this animal swimming in the water? Is it a frog or a toad? It's hard to tell the two apart. They are alike in many ways.

Both the frog and the toad lay eggs in the water. The babies that grow from the eggs are called tadpoles. Tadpoles have tails that help them swim. Then they lose their tails. This happens as they grow into frogs or toads. ②

---

① **Text Features**
MAKING PREDICTIONS

- Titles can often help you make predictions about what the selection will be about. Point to the title. What does the title tell you about what you might learn in this article? *(the differences betweeen frogs and toads)*

② **Language Features**
WORDS USED TO COMPARE AND CONTRAST

- Did anyone notice the word *both* in the second paragraph? Do you think *both* is used to compare things that are alike, or things that are different? *(alike)* Why do you think this?

How They Look

A frog has smooth, sticky skin. It mostly lives in water. A frog's skin has to stay a little wet, or moist. A frog also has long back legs. Long legs help a frog leap far. The feet on a frog's back legs are webbed. The skin between a frog's toes helps it swim.

Frog

Toad

A toad is different. It has a short, fat body. A toad's skin is dry and bumpy. It spends more time on land than in water. A toad's feet are webbed like a frog's. But a toad's legs are different because they are much shorter. Instead of leaping, a toad walks or hops. ③

3

③ **Conceptual Meaning**
COMPARING AND CONTRASTING

■ Let's think about what we read about frogs and toads. What are some things that are alike about frogs and toads? *(Both have webbed feet.)*

■ What are some things that are different? *(Frogs have smooth, sticky skin. Toads have short, fat bodies. Frogs live mostly in water. Toads spend more time on land. Frogs have long back legs to leap with. Toads' legs are shorter to walk or hop.)*

ENGLISH LANGUAGE LEARNERS

Show children the phrase "spends more time" in the second paragraph. Explain that this means that a toad lives mostly on land, but sometimes goes into the water. Have children create sentences in which they use the phrase "spend more time" to compare and contrast the length of time devoted to various activities in a typical day or class period.

■ How does poison keep the toad safe? The answer to this question is not really given in the paragraph. Instead, you have to use the other information in the paragraph to figure out the answer. *(Animals who eat the toad will get sick and learn not to eat it again.)*

How They Stay Safe

Toad

The color of a toad helps it stay safe. A toad is brown and gray. It looks like the mud it lives in. An animal that wants to eat a toad may not be able to see it.

A toad also stays safe because it has a sack of poison behind each eye. When a toad is afraid, poison leaks out of the sack. Animals who eat the toad will get sick. ④

poison sack

bulging eyes

Frog

Like a toad, a frog uses its color to stay safe. However, most frogs are green and brown. They look like the water they live in.

A frog's eyes help it stay safe, too. The eyes bulge out on top of its head. A frog can see all around because its eyes stick out so far. When the frog's body is underwater, the frog's eyes can still see above the water. The frog can look for danger. Then it can leap or swim away to safety.

4

Toad

bumpy skin

poison sack

short legs

webbed feet

What titles should go in these boxes?

Frog

bulging eyes

smooth, sticky skin

webbed feet

long legs

Now that you know the difference between a frog and a toad, look at the animal below. Is it a frog or a toad? ❺

? ● frog ○ toad

5

- Look at the diagrams of the frog and toad. They show us what frogs and toads look like. Using the diagrams to help you, can you figure out whether the picture below is of a frog or toad? *(It is a frog.)*

- Point to the lines that connect a part of the picture to a word. These words are called labels. They name the part of the picture the line points to. How many labels does each picture have? *(four)*

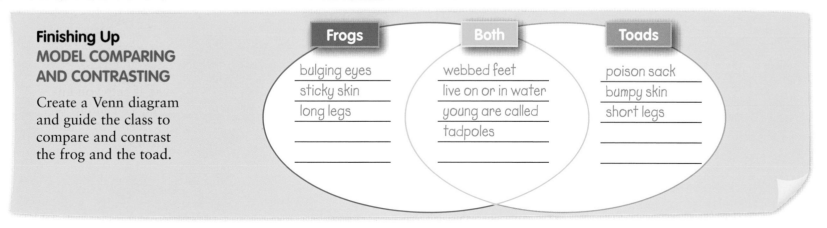

Finishing Up
MODEL COMPARING AND CONTRASTING

Create a Venn diagram and guide the class to compare and contrast the frog and the toad.

Frogs	Both	Toads
bulging eyes	webbed feet	poison sack
sticky skin	live on or in water	bumpy skin
long legs	young are called	short legs
	tadpoles	

Comprehension Focus
MAKING INFERENCES

An inference is a guess based on clues in the text. Tell children that authors often include clues in their writing that can help readers understand things that are not directly stated. As they read, children should use these clues, along with what they already know, to help them make inferences.

VOCABULARY

The following words appear in the story. Explain them briefly as you come to them: *decorate,* add things to make something look good; *tide,* the force that brings water to and from the shore.

The Mystery of the Missing Shell

① Will: This may be the best sand castle we've ever built, Beth! I'm glad your dad told us to pack the sand down first to make a strong foundation for it to sit on.

Beth: The moat is my favorite part. Every sand castle needs water around it. The moat will help protect it. There are a lot of crabs on the beach today! **②**

Will: Let's find a shell to decorate our castle.

Beth: This shell will look perfect on top. Let's show my dad.

(Beth and Will get Beth's dad.)

6

① Text Features
DIALOGUE

- In a play, the names of the characters are shown to the left side of the lines they say. Their words do not appear in quotation marks as in a regular story. Point to the names of the characters who speak on this page. What are their names? *(Will and Beth)*

② Text Features
PICTURES

- Look at the picture on this page. How can it help you understand what a moat is? *(The picture shows a channel dug around the outside of the sand castle. It's filled with water. The picture matches the description in the text.)*

Beth: What do you think, Dad?

Dad: That's a great sand castle! You two must have worked really hard. But where did those animal tracks come from?

Will: Wait a minute! Where is our shell? It's missing! ❸

Beth: I can't believe it! The shell was just here. Where did it go?

Dad: The tide didn't take it. Your whole castle would have washed away.

Will: The wind didn't blow it away. That shell was stuck into the sand castle.

Beth: Someone wouldn't pick it up. There are plenty of other shells on the beach.

What do you think happened to the shell?

■ What do you think happened to the shell? *(Maybe it walked away.)* What clues did you use to help you decide? *(Dad saw animal tracks where the shell had been.)*

4 **Implicit Meaning**
MAKING INFERENCES

■ Will says that the shell could not just walk away. Do you think he is right? Why or why not? *(No, shells with animals living inside can move.)*

Will: Let's get another one. Here's one that looks almost the same.

(Will puts another shell on the castle.)

Dad: Now who is going to be the last one to jump into the surf with me?

(Dad, Beth, and Will splash into the waves. Then they all walk from the water back to the sand castle.)

Beth: Look! The shell is gone again!

Dad: That is strange. Where could that shell be?

Will: Let's look for it. It couldn't just walk away. **4**

What do you think happened to the second shell?

8

(Beth, Dad, and Will walk down the beach.)

Beth: Will, did you say that our shell couldn't just walk away? Maybe it did. Look over there! It looks like our shells are walking down the beach. ⑤

Will: Those shells must have had hermit crabs inside of them. I guess a crab's shell is its home. It doesn't need to live in our castle!

9

⑤ **Conceptual Meaning**

ANIMAL CHARACTERISTICS

■ What are some ways that animals can move? How do hermit crab move? *(Animals can fly, crawl, walk, swim, run. Hermit crabs walk on their legs.)*

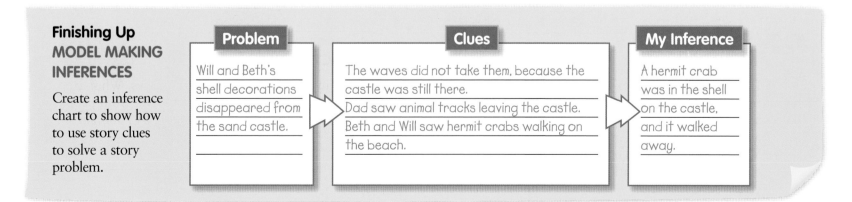

Finishing Up

MODEL MAKING INFERENCES

Create an inference chart to show how to use story clues to solve a story problem.

Problem	Clues	My Inference
Will and Beth's shell decorations disappeared from the sand castle.	The waves did not take them, because the castle was still there. Dad saw animal tracks leaving the castle. Beth and Will saw hermit crabs walking on the beach.	A hermit crab was in the shell on the castle, and it walked away.

Comprehension Focus
COMPARING AND CONTRASTING

Remind children that articles may compare by telling how things are alike. They may contrast by telling how things are different. Suggest that children think about how different creatures are alike or different as they read this article.

VOCABULARY

The following words appear in the story. Explain them briefly as you come to them: *warning*, danger sign; *attacks*, bothers or harms; *bands*, colored stripes.

LESSON 3

Warning Signs

If an ant attacks me, I spit something sticky at it!

Ladybug

If I bite you, it will feel like you are on fire!

Fire ant

10

What do you do when you see a **RED** light? Stop!

What do you do when you see a **YELLOW** light? Stop, because the light will soon be red.

What do you do when you see a **GREEN** light? Go! ❶

Did you know that some animals use colors this way, too? The way they look sends messages to other animals. Their bright colors are a warning sign for people and animals to stay far away.

In nature, bright colors like red and yellow often mean "Stop! Don't eat me or you will be sorry!" Some brightly colored animals have poison in them. Sometimes they just taste really bad. Some of them sting anything that attacks them. ❷

Poison dart frog

❶ **Text Features**
PUNCTUATION

■ Did you notice all the exclamation marks on this page? This mark shows excitement. It tells you to read a sentence with special importance. Who can show how to read the sentences with an exclamation mark?

❷ **Conceptual Meaning**
ANIMAL CHARACTERISTICS

■ Animals use many signals to protect themselves. What are some ways that animals can protect themselves from people or other animals? *(with poison, by stinging, by having a bad taste)*

Pretend that you are an animal that hunts other animals for food. Would you want to eat a green animal or a red animal? If you ate the green animal, you would probably have a good snack. If you ate the red animal, you might get a surprise! ❸

The colors of these animals are bright to make sure that other animals get the message to stay away. These animals need to look special, and they do! ❹

Bee

We have stingers and we're not afraid to use them!

Wasp

Don't try to eat me! I will spit out something that tastes bad.

Foaming grasshopper

11

❸ **Implicit Meaning**
MAKING INFERENCES

■ An animal's color can tell whether or not it is safe to eat. What kind of surprise might you get if you ate a red animal? *(The red animal might taste bad or be filled with poison.)* Why do you think this? *(Red means stop.)*

❹ **Text Features**
SPEECH BALOONS

■ Notice the words inside the speech balloons by the pictures of the bee, wasp, and grasshopper. Do you think they would really say these words? *(No, insects don't talk.)* Why are these words shown in a speech balloon? *(These are messages that the colors of the insects are sending.)*

ENGLISH LANGUAGE LEARNERS

Explain that the phrase, "You will be sorry" is often used to warn someone not to do something. Ask children to list some things they might warn someone about. Then have them use the phrase in a sentence: *(You will be sorry if you _____.)* Prompt children with examples such as, "don't study for the quiz" or "go out in the rain without your raincoat."

PICTURES AND CAPTIONS

■ Pictures can help us to understand what we read. The words on this page explain how to tell a milk snake from a coral snake. Point to the picture that shows red bands touching yellow bands. Is this the coral snake or the milk snake? *(coral snake)* Is it poisonous? *(yes)* Now point to the snake with red bands touching black bands. Is this the coral snake or the milk snake? *(milk snake)* Is it safe? *(yes)*

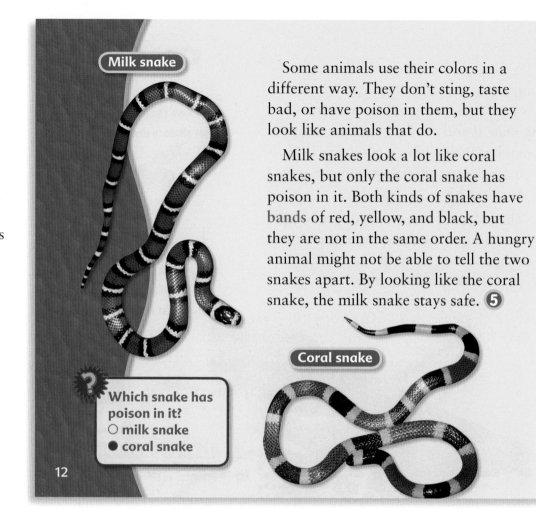

Milk snake

Coral snake

Which snake has poison in it?
○ milk snake
● coral snake

12

Some animals use their colors in a different way. They don't sting, taste bad, or have poison in them, but they look like animals that do.

Milk snakes look a lot like coral snakes, but only the coral snake has poison in it. Both kinds of snakes have **bands** of red, yellow, and black, but they are not in the same order. A hungry animal might not be able to tell the two snakes apart. By looking like the coral snake, the milk snake stays safe. ⑤

The viceroy butterfly and the monarch butterfly are both orange and black. But only the monarch butterfly has poison in it. Can you tell these butterflies apart? The viceroy has stripes near the bottom of its wings. Do you think a hungry bird could tell them apart? **6**

Many animals use their colors as warning signs. Now that you know what they mean, you can follow the warning signs, too. When you see a brightly colored animal, stay away!

Monarch butterfly

Viceroy butterfly

? How are these butterflies the same?

13

6 Implicit Meaning
MAKING INFERENCES

- The viceroy butterfly and the monarch butterfly look a lot alike. How does this help protect the viceroy butterfly? *(Animals may think the viceroy butterfly is a bad-tasting monarch butterfly because they look alike.)*

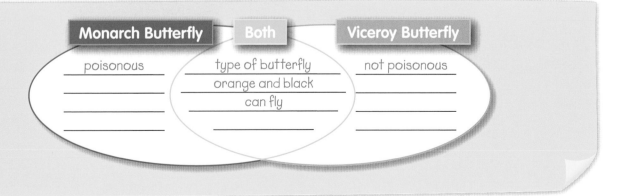

Finishing Up
MODEL COMPARING AND CONTRASTING

Create a Venn diagram to guide children in comparing and contrasting a monarch butterfly with a viceroy butterfly.

Monarch Butterfly	Both	Viceroy Butterfly
poisonous	type of butterfly	not poisonous
	orange and black	
	can fly	

Comprehension Focus

IDENTIFYING FACT AND OPINION

Tell children that facts are statements that can be proved. Opinions are what people think or believe. Encourage children to look for facts and opinions as they read *Amazing Animals*.

VOCABULARY

The following words appear in the story. Explain them briefly as you come to them: *interesting*, something you want to know more about; *tiny*, very small; *prey*, an animal hunted by another animal for food.

LESSON
4

Amazing Animals

What are the most amazing things on Earth? I think animals are! Do you know about the world's fastest animals? What about the smallest and the biggest animals? I feel that these are the most interesting animals of all. **1** **2**

14

---

1 Explicit Meaning
IDENTIFYING FACT AND OPINION

■ In the author's opinion, what kinds of animals are most interesting? (*the world's fastest, biggest, and smallest animals*)

2 Implicit Meaning
MAKING CONNECTIONS

■ In your opinion, what are some interesting kinds of animals? Why are they interesting?

The World's Fastest Animals

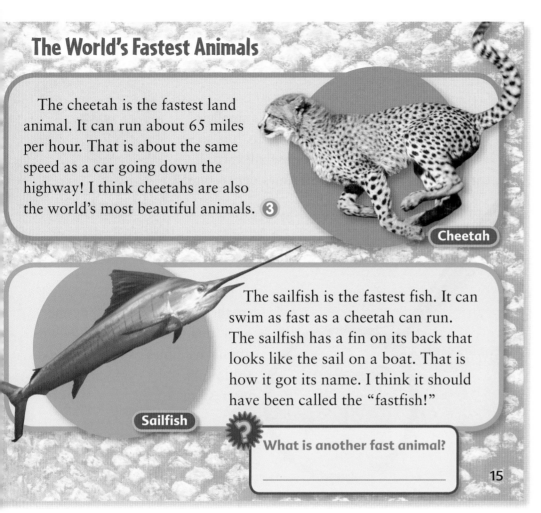

The cheetah is the fastest land animal. It can run about 65 miles per hour. That is about the same speed as a car going down the highway! I think cheetahs are also the world's most beautiful animals. ③

Cheetah

The sailfish is the fastest fish. It can swim as fast as a cheetah can run. The sailfish has a fin on its back that looks like the sail on a boat. That is how it got its name. I think it should have been called the "fastfish!"

Sailfish

What is another fast animal?

_____

15

③ **Language Features**

WORDS USED TO SHOW FACTS AND OPINIONS

- Which sentence in the first paragraph shows an opinion? *(I think cheetahs are also the world's most beautiful animals.)*

- What words help you know that this is an opinion? *(I think)*

④ Text Features

PICTURES

■ Look at the rulers on this page. What do they show? *(How small the animals are.)*

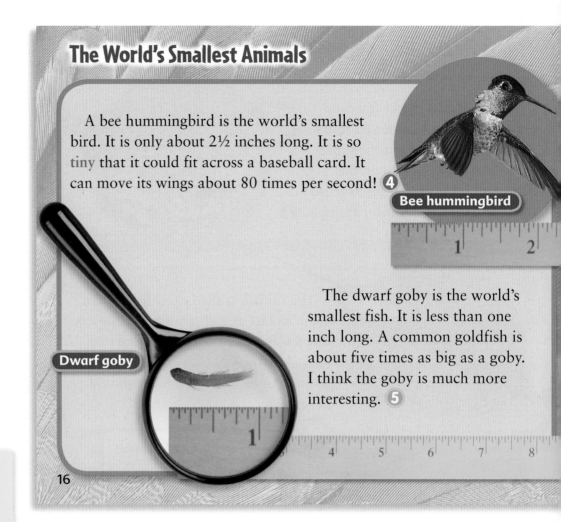

The World's Smallest Animals

A bee hummingbird is the world's smallest bird. It is only about 2½ inches long. It is so tiny that it could fit across a baseball card. It can move its wings about 80 times per second! ④

Bee hummingbird

The dwarf goby is the world's smallest fish. It is less than one inch long. A common goldfish is about five times as big as a goby. I think the goby is much more interesting. ⑤

Dwarf goby

16

⑤ Conceptual Meaning

MAKING CONNECTIONS

■ Have you ever seen a goldfish? Can you imagine how small a dwarf goby must be? Do you agree with the author's opinion that the dwarf goby is more interesting?

The World's Largest Animals

Goliath spider

The world's largest spider is the Goliath spider. It can grow to be almost one foot long! These spiders live in rain forests. They attack insects and some small reptiles.

Python

The world's longest snake is a kind of python. This snake wraps around its prey. Then it squeezes it. This snake is almost as long as a school bus! I think the biggest animals are the best animals.

What animal do you think is the best animal?

_____

17

Finishing Up
MODEL IDENTIFYING FACT AND OPINION

Create a fact and opinion chart to help children identify facts and opinions in the article.

Facts About Interesting Animals	Opinions About Interesting Animals
The cheetah is the fastest land animal.	I think it should have been called the "fast fish!"
A sailfish is the fastest fish.	I think the biggest animals are the best animals.

Comprehension Focus
IDENTIFYING MAIN IDEA AND DETAILS

Tell children that articles usually have a main idea and details. The main idea tells what the article is mostly about. Details give more information about the main idea. As they read, children should try to identify the main idea and details. This will help them understand the most important parts of the article.

VOCABULARY

The following words appear in the story. Explain them briefly as you come to them: *discovered,* found; *fossils,* traces of plants or animals that lived long ago; *skull,* the bones in an animal's head.

LESSON
5

MEET SUE, THE T. REX WONDER

A grown person is not nearly as tall as a T. rex.

18

Meet Sue! Sue is a Tyrannosaurus rex (tuh RAN uh sor us REX). Sue is a dinosaur that lived long ago. She is named for the person who discovered her bones. Sue's bones give clues about the past. ❶

❶ **Explicit Meaning**
UNDERSTANDING DETAILS

■ Have you ever heard of a dinosaur named Sue? Why is she called that? *(Because the person who found her was named Sue.)*

Looking for Clues

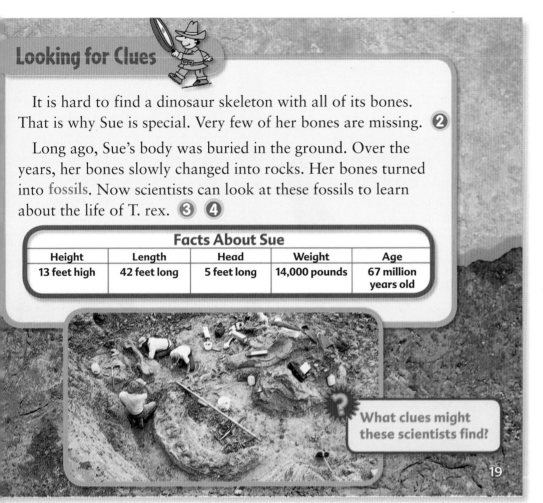

It is hard to find a dinosaur skeleton with all of its bones. That is why Sue is special. Very few of her bones are missing. ❷

Long ago, Sue's body was buried in the ground. Over the years, her bones slowly changed into rocks. Her bones turned into fossils. Now scientists can look at these fossils to learn about the life of T. rex. ❸ ❹

Facts About Sue

Height	Length	Head	Weight	Age
13 feet high	42 feet long	5 feet long	14,000 pounds	67 million years old

What clues might these scientists find?

19

❷ **Explicit Meaning**
UNDERSTANDING DETAILS

■ Why is Sue special? *(Because very few of her bones are missing.)*

❸ **Language Features**
VOCABULARY

■ Sue's bones turned into fossils. Who can tell me what a fossil is? *(a trace of plants or animals that lived long ago, set in rock)*

❹ **Text Features**
READING CHARTS

■ Now let's look at this chart to find out more information about Sue. Sue was really big and lived a long, long time ago. How tall was Sue? *(13 feet high.)* How long ago did Sue live? *(67 million years ago.)*

Meet Sue, The T. Rex Wonder   **19**

⑤ Implicit Meaning
MAKING INFERENCES

■ Scientists compared Sue's teeth to the teeth of animals that are alive today. Why did they do this? *(Because they believed that Sue might share characteristics with animals that are alive today.)* What did they find? *(That Sue ate meat because she had the same kind of teeth as meat eaters.)* Let's look for more of these clues as we read the rest of the story.

ENGLISH LANGUAGE LEARNERS

To help children learn about sense words, call their attention to the words "see, hear, smell, taste, and feel." Explain that you see with your eyes, hear with your ears, smell with your nose, taste with your tongue, and feel with your skin. Ask children to say the words while pointing to the corresponding body part. Then ask them to use both words in a sentence. *(My eyes see a friend. My nose smells a flower.)*

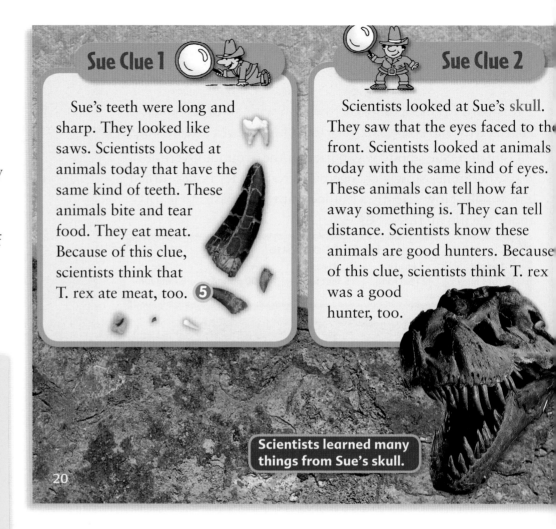

Sue Clue 1

Sue's teeth were long and sharp. They looked like saws. Scientists looked at animals today that have the same kind of teeth. These animals bite and tear food. They eat meat. Because of this clue, scientists think that T. rex ate meat, too. ⑤

Sue Clue 2

Scientists looked at Sue's skull. They saw that the eyes faced to the front. Scientists looked at animals today with the same kind of eyes. These animals can tell how far away something is. They can tell distance. Scientists know these animals are good hunters. Because of this clue, scientists think T. rex was a good hunter, too.

Scientists learned many things from Sue's skull.

20

Sue Clue 3

Scientists looked inside Sue's skull. They looked where her brain once was. A brain has parts to help animals see, hear, smell, taste, and feel. They found that one part of Sue's brain was very large. Scientists looked at animals today that have the same kind of brain. These animals have a good sense of smell. Because of this clue, scientists think T. rex had a good sense of smell, too.

Scientists are still learning more about Sue and other dinosaurs like her. Sue will keep giving us clues about the past. **6**

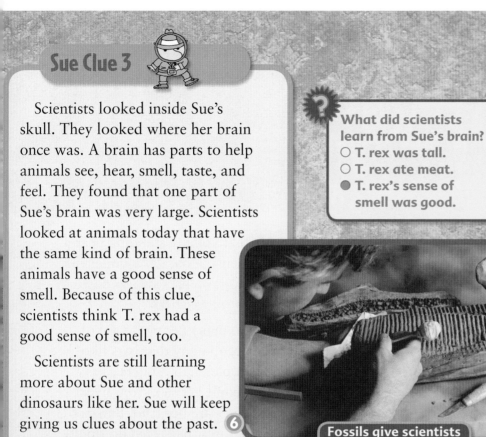

?

What did scientists learn from Sue's brain?
○ T. rex was tall.
○ T. rex ate meat.
● T. rex's sense of smell was good.

Fossils give scientists clues about the past.

21

6 Implicit Meaning
IDENTIFYING MAIN IDEA

■ A main idea may be stated in a few places in an article. The title often tells the main idea. The first paragraph may show it, too. Often the main idea is restated at the end of the article. What main idea sentence can you find at the end of the article? *(Sue will keep giving us clues about the past.)*

Finishing Up
MODEL IDENTIFYING MAIN IDEA AND DETAILS

Complete a main idea and detail chart with children to review important ideas in the article. When they're done, ask children to draw a picture of Sue's bones.

Main Idea	Details
Sue's bones give clues about the past.	Her long sharp teeth show that the T. rex ate meat.
	Her skull shows that she was a good hunter.
	She could tell distance. She had a good sense of smell.

Comprehension Focus
RECOGNIZING AUTHOR'S PURPOSE

Explain that authors often write to entertain readers, to inform them, or to get them to think a certain way. Tell children that as they read the article, they should think about why the author wrote it.

VOCABULARY

The following words appear in the story. Explain them briefly as you come to them: *darts,* moves quickly and suddenly; *mammals,* animals that have hair or fur and have live babies; *echo,* sound caused by a noise reflecting off a surface; *pollen,* powder made by flowers to make new flowers.

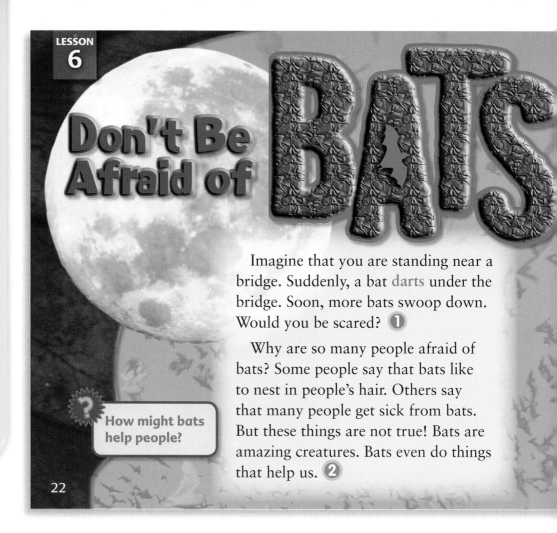

Imagine that you are standing near a bridge. Suddenly, a bat **darts** under the bridge. Soon, more bats swoop down. Would you be scared? **1**

Why are so many people afraid of bats? Some people say that bats like to nest in people's hair. Others say that many people get sick from bats. But these things are not true! Bats are amazing creatures. Bats even do things that help us. **2**

How might bats help people?

22

1 Language Features
RECOGNIZING AUTHOR'S STYLE

■ At the beginning of this paragraph, the author asks you to use your imagination. Is it hard to imagine what the author describes?

2 Implicit Meaning
IDENTIFYING AUTHOR'S PURPOSE

■ Read the last two sentences on this page. Can you tell how the author feels about bats? *(The author likes bats.)*

Amazing Bats

Bats are mammals. They have fur. Their babies are born live. Mother bats make milk. Bats are the only mammals that can fly. ③

Many bats fly by using sound to help them find their way. The bat makes a little noise. Then it listens. The sound hits an object and bounces back to the bat. The echo tells the bat where things are. Then the bat knows where to go. ④

How can sound help this bat?

23

③ **Conceptual Meaning**
MAKING CONNECTIONS

■ Point to the word *mammal*. Let's review the things that make bats mammals: They have fur, their babies are born live, and their mothers make milk. From these traits, can you name other mammals? *(dogs, cats, people)*

④ **Language Features**
VOCABULARY

■ What happens when something you say echoes? *(It sounds like what you said is repeated over and over.)*

■ What are some places you might hear an echo? *(in a cave; in a big empty room)*

- What are two good things we learned about bats on this page? *(They help some plants grow. They eat lots of insects.)*

Bats Help Us

Do you like to eat bananas? If so, you might thank a bat. Some bats help bananas, dates, and figs grow. Plants need pollen to grow. Like bees, bats move pollen from one plant to another.

Do you like to get bitten by insects? Of course you don't. You might thank a bat for eating insects. Most bats eat insects that are pests to people. One bat can eat up to 600 insects in one hour! ⑤

Short-tailed fruit bat

24

⑥ Implicit Meaning
IDENTIFYING MAIN IDEA

- Summarize the author's main point on this page. *(Bats can be helpful to humans in many ways.)*

Bats Around the World

The number of bats in the world is getting smaller. As people build cities and roads, bats are losing their homes. Some people try to harm bats. They think that all bats are pests. But now you know that bats are really amazing creatures that help people.

In fact, you may come to think of bats the way people do in China. In China, bats are thought to bring good luck and happiness.

No matter where you are in the world, don't be afraid of bats. If you see a bat, don't scream. Just think of how lucky you are! **7**

Flying foxes

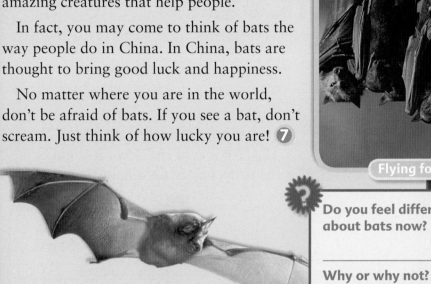

? Do you feel differently about bats now?

_____

Why or why not?

25

7 Implicit Meaning
IDENTIFYING AUTHOR'S PURPOSE

- Why does the author suggest that you think about bats the way people in China do? *(People in China like bats; the author thinks you should like bats, too.)*

ENGLISH LANGUAGE LEARNERS

Call children's attention to the phrase "bats are thought to bring good luck and happiness." Tell them that the phrase "thought to bring" means that "people think or believe this." Ask children to think of other things that people believe. Have them use a similar phrase to state their ideas. *(A black cat is thought to bring bad luck.)*

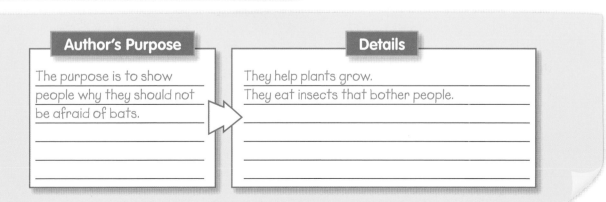

Finishing Up
MODEL RECOGNIZING AUTHOR'S PURPOSE

Create a chart to help children recognize the author's purpose in writing the article.

Author's Purpose

The purpose is to show people why they should not be afraid of bats.

Details

They help plants grow.
They eat insects that bother people.

Comprehension Focus
IDENTIFYING CAUSE AND EFFECT

Tell children that causes tell what makes something happen. Effects show what happens as a result. Explain that looking for causes and effects will help them better understand what they read. Encourage them to look for causes and effects as they read the story.

VOCABULARY

The following words appear in the story. Explain them briefly as you come to them: *reporters,* people who tell the news; *exist,* to live or be real; *prove,* to show that something is true.

Is the Loch Ness Monster Real?

Is the Loch Ness Monster real? Reporters often visit a village in Scotland to find out. The small town sits on the shore of a lake called Loch Ness. The lake is cold and deep. It could be the perfect place for a monster to hide. ❶

What do you think this picture shows?

the monster

Why do you think so?

26

❶ **Explicit Meaning**
IDENTIFYING CAUSE AND EFFECT

■ Do you see a cause and effect in this first paragraph? Why do reporters often visit Loch Ness in Scotland? *(to find out if the Loch Ness monster is real)*

The Loch Ness Monster is also called Nessie. Nessie is a very old character. Stories have been told about her for about 1,500 years.

Over time, there have been thousands of sightings of the monster. Could they all be wrong? Many people now visit Scotland because they have heard tales of the monster. But does the Loch Ness Monster really exist? ② ③

② **Language Features**

WORDS USED TO SHOW CAUSE AND EFFECT

- Point to the word *because* in the second paragraph. Is the word because used to show a cause or effect? *(cause)*

- Read the rest of the sentence. What is the effect in this sentence? *(People go to Scotland)* What is the cause in this sentence? *(They have heard tales of the monster.)*

③ **Text Features**

PICTURES

- Let's look at the newspaper clippings on this page. Read the headlines. Do you think these clippings prove whether the monster exists? Why or why not? *(Yes, because news articles tell facts. No, the headlines don't show that the articles prove anything.)*

④ Explicit Meaning
UNDERSTANDING CAUSE AND EFFECT

■ Why did the photograph make more people believe in Nessie? *(A lot of people believe what they see, even if it is not what it seems to be.)*

Some people thought Nessie looked like this.

What might prove that Nessie is real?

Photos like this one caused some people to believe in Nessie.

Many people have tried to spot Nessie. One man said he had a photo of her. The photo became famous. It seemed to **prove** the monster was real, so people believed in Nessie more than ever. It was a trick, though. Years later, people found out the photo was fake. ④

Another man said he had caught Nessie on film, too. There was something moving in his film. But no one could prove that it was a lake monster. Some people had trouble believing him. ⑤

⑤ Text Features
PICTURES AND CAPTIONS

■ Many of the pictures in this article have captions. These sentences show what is important for you to know about the pictures. What does this caption explain? *(It identifies the photo that caused many people to believe in Nessie.)*

What are people really seeing in the lake? No one can say for sure. Some people believe that it is a monster. But this cannot be proven.

Other people think it is a kind of dinosaur. But why would it still be living today? Still others think it might be a giant otter. But why aren't there other giant otters in the world? Some scientists say it could be waves pushing things up from under the water. But other scientists do not agree.

For now, Nessie is one of the world's greatest mysteries. Each year people go to Scotland to try to solve it. What do you think they will find in the deep, dark lake? ⑥

Many people have tried to find Nessie.

Loch Ness, Scotland

29

⑥ **Conceptual Meaning**
IDENTIFYING CAUSE AND EFFECT

- Why do you think so many people tell stories about Nessie? *(People like mysteries about unusual creatures.)*

- Why do you think so many people visit Loch Ness? *(They want to see for themselves if the monster is real or not. They are hoping to see the monster.)*

ENGLISH LANGUAGE LEARNERS

Tell children that the word *sightings* means "times people believe they have seen something." Encourage volunteers to tell of sightings in the night sky or around their community that they may have heard about or witnessed first hand.

Finishing Up
MODEL IDENTIFYING CAUSE AND EFFECT

Create a cause and effect chart to connect causes and effects in the article.

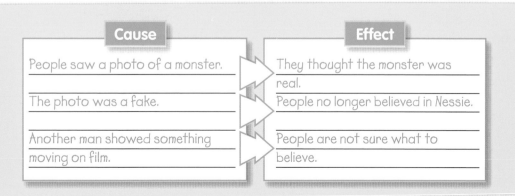

Cause	Effect
People saw a photo of a monster.	They thought the monster was real.
The photo was a fake.	People no longer believed in Nessie.
Another man showed something moving on film.	People are not sure what to believe.

LESSON 8

Comprehension Focus
MAKING PREDICTIONS

Tell children that as they read, they can use story clues to help them make predictions, or guesses about what will happen next. Encourage them to make predictions as they read this story in order to stay focused on what they are reading.

VOCABULARY

The following words appear in the story. Explain them briefly as you come to them: *brag,* to speak highly of yourself; *embarrassed,* feel shy or guilty about something; *hibernate,* spend the winter in a deep sleep.

LESSON 8

WHY BEARS SLEEP THROUGH WINTER

A Native American Legend ❶

Bear was proud. He would brag all the time. "I'm the biggest and the strongest animal in the forest!" he said. The other animals did not argue with Bear because it was true. ❷

One day Bear ran down a snowy hill faster than the wind. He stopped beside a frozen lake and began to brag as usual. "I'm the fastest animal in the forest," he said.

Then a little voice said, "No, you're not! I'm faster!" It was Turtle.

30

❶ Conceptual Meaning

MAKING PREDICTIONS

- This story is a Native American legend. Legends often try to explain something about nature. What event in nature do you think this story will be about? *(Why bears sleep in the winter)*

❷ Text Features

PUNCTUATION

- What do these quotation marks in this paragraph show you? *(These are the words Bear said.)*

Bear and Turtle decided to race to see who was faster. Bear would run around the edge of the lake, and Turtle would swim.

Bear asked, "How do I know that you will swim all around the lake? You could just swim straight across. I can't see you under the ice."

Turtle answered, "We can make three holes in the ice. I'll stick my head through each hole to show you where I am."

Then Turtle went to talk to his brother and sister. He had a plan. ③

Do you think Turtle or Bear will win the race?

_____

Why?

31

③ **Implicit Meaning**
MAKING PREDICTIONS

■ What do you predict Turtle will do? *(He may try to trick Bear.)* Why do you think so? *(Because the story says that turtle has a plan.)*

■ Why do you think Turtle talks to his brother and sister? *(They are going to help him win the race.)*

4 Conceptual Meaning
MAKING CONNECTIONS

- If two people were having a race and one of them was always bragging, which one would you want to win the race? *(The one who did not always brag.)*

What do you think Turtle did to win the race?

All the animals came to watch the race. They wanted Turtle to win so that Bear would stop bragging. 4

Elk punched holes in the ice. Then Fox yelled "Go!" Turtle dove under the ice. Bear began to run. Soon, Turtle poked his head through the first hole.

He called, "Bear, I'm faster!" 5

Bear began to run faster. Turtle poked his head through the second hole.

He called, "Bear, I'm faster!" Turtle was getting farther ahead.

Bear ran even faster. But before long, Turtle poked his head out of the last hole. He had won the race. Turtle was the fastest!

32

5 Explicit Meaning
UNDERSTANDING DETAILS

- Why did Elk punch holes in the ice? *(Because Bear did not trust that Turtle would race all the way around the lake. He wanted to see him during the race.)*

Bear was **embarrassed** that he had lost the race to such a little animal. He was very tired, too. Bear went back to his cave after the race. He slept for the rest of the winter.

After all of the animals had left, Turtle rapped on the ice with his hand. A head popped up through each hole.

"Thank you, brother and sister!" Turtle said. "We may be slow, but we are very smart!"

To this day, bears **hibernate** each year. They sleep through the winter so they will not remember the race.

33

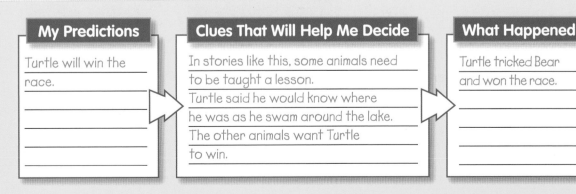

Finishing Up
MODEL MAKING PREDICTIONS

Create a prediction chart to guide children through clues that help them make and confirm their predictions.

My Predictions	Clues That Will Help Me Decide	What Happened
Turtle will win the race.	In stories like this, some animals need to be taught a lesson. Turtle said he would know where he was as he swam around the lake. The other animals want Turtle to win.	Turtle tricked Bear and won the race.

Comprehension Focus
SEQUENCING

Tell children that when they put events in order, they are sequencing. Understanding and recalling the order of events in a story or a process is a good way to remember it. Ask children to look for words that show order as they read.

VOCABULARY

The following words appear in the article. Explain them briefly as you come to them: *magma,* liquid rock inside a volcano; *erupts,* burst out suddenly; *lava,* liquid burning rock that comes out of a volcano.

LESSON
9

Volcano
A Mountain of Fire

A volcano is a kind of mountain. The mountain has a hole on top. The hole leads deep inside the earth. It is very hot inside the earth. It is so hot that rocks melt and become liquid. This melted rock is called magma.

A volcano erupts when magma bursts out of the mountain. How does a volcano erupt into a mountain of fire? ❶

34

❶ **Language Features**
VOCABULARY

■ Look at the first sentence of this paragraph. What words tell you about the meaning of the word erupts? *(bursts out)*

First, the magma forms a pool. ❷

All magma has gas inside it. The gas starts to push the magma up from inside the earth. The magma forms a large pool deep inside the volcano. ❸

ash cloud

hole

lava

Magma pushes up from inside the earth to form a volcano.

magma pool

35

❷ **Text Features**
HEADINGS

■ Point to the heading on this page. It tells what happens first inside a volcano before it erupts. What do you predict the next heading will show? *(what happens next inside the volcano)*

❸ **Text Features**
READING DIAGRAMS

■ Look at the diagram of an erupting volcano. Let's read the labeled parts. What label is at the top of the volcano? *(ash cloud)* What others parts of the volcano have labels? *(hole, lava, magma pool)* How do the labels help you? *(They tell you what the parts of the volcano are called.)*

UNDERSTANDING CAUSE AND EFFECT

■ So, after the volcano fills up with magma, the magma hardens. Why does the gas get trapped inside the volcano? *(because the magma cools and hardens on the top of the mountain and stops the gasses from escaping)*

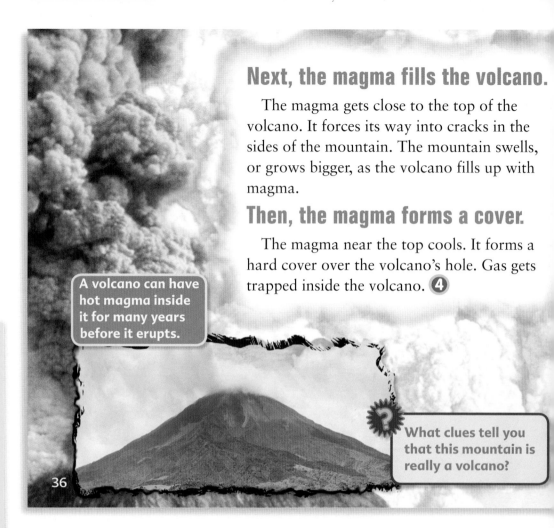

Next, the magma fills the volcano.

The magma gets close to the top of the volcano. It forces its way into cracks in the sides of the mountain. The mountain swells, or grows bigger, as the volcano fills up with magma.

Then, the magma forms a cover.

The magma near the top cools. It forms a hard cover over the volcano's hole. Gas gets trapped inside the volcano. ④

A volcano can have hot magma inside it for many years before it erupts.

36

What clues tell you that this mountain is really a volcano?

Last, the volcano erupts. ⑤

The gas breaks through the hard cover. The gas also breaks through the sides. Rock, magma, and ash fly into the sky. ⑥

Soon magma flows from the volcano. It becomes lava. Lava is bright orange. It moves down the mountain. It burns everything in its way. The volcano now looks like a mountain of fire!

Lava from a volcano burns everything in its path.

In what order do these things happen?

_3_ Magma forms a hard cover.

_1_ Magma forms a pool.

_4_ The volcano erupts.

_2_ Magma fills the volcano.

37

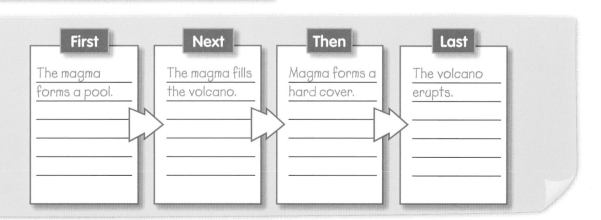

First	Next	Then	Last
The magma forms a pool.	The magma fills the volcano.	Magma forms a hard cover.	The volcano erupts.

Comprehension Focus
IDENTIFYING CAUSE AND EFFECT

Remind children that a cause is what makes something happen. An effect shows what happens as a result. Tell children to look for causes and effects of changes on Earth as they read.

VOCABULARY

The following words appear in the article. Explain them briefly as you come to them: *landforms,* mountains, valleys, and other features of Earth; *processes,* sets of steps that cause a change; *erosion,* act of wind, water, or ice wearing away rock or soil.

Our Changing Earth

From space, planet Earth looks like a smooth ball. But up close, it is not smooth at all. Earth is covered with different landforms, from the tallest mountains to the deepest valleys. The land looks different today than it did hundreds of years ago. Our planet is changing every day. **1**

38

1 **Language Features**
COMPARING WORDS

■ Point to the words *tallest and deepest.* We use words like these to describe the look, size, or shape of things. Words that end in *–est* usually compare three or more other things. What things are being compared here? *(mountains, valleys)*

Every place on Earth looks different. But there are only two **processes** that make all of the landforms on Earth. In the first process, large pieces of Earth's crust crash together or pull apart. This process can make mountains, volcanoes, or large cracks. In the second process, wind, water, or ice wear away pieces of rock and soil. This process is called **erosion**. Over hundreds of years, erosion can shape even the hardest rock. ②

This island was made by a volcano, but it is slowly wearing away into sand.

39

MAKING INFERENCES

■ The processes that shape Earth's landforms happen so slowly that we can't see them. How might the land in this photograph have looked a million years ago? How might it look a million years in the future?

UNDERSTANDING CAUSE AND EFFECT

- What turns mountains into sand? *(wind and rain)*

- What might have formed the valley shown in the photograph? *(The river may have carved out the valley over time.)*

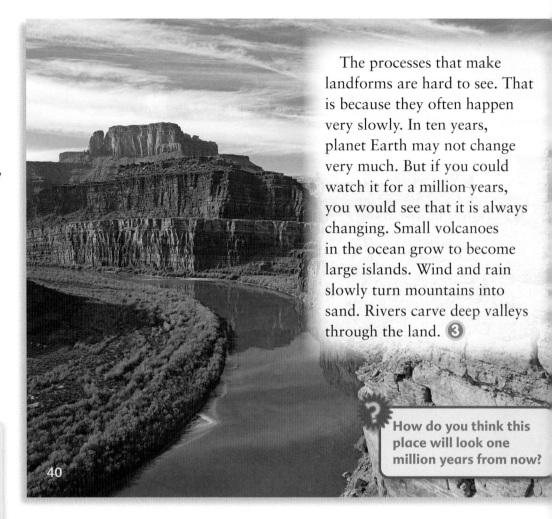

The processes that make landforms are hard to see. That is because they often happen very slowly. In ten years, planet Earth may not change very much. But if you could watch it for a million years, you would see that it is always changing. Small volcanoes in the ocean grow to become large islands. Wind and rain slowly turn mountains into sand. Rivers carve deep valleys through the land. ③

40

How do you think this place will look one million years from now?

How Mountains Are Made

Mountains are made in different ways. Volcanic mountains are made when volcanoes erupt. Lava piles up again and again, making the mountain grow bigger. Block mountains are made when the ground moves and huge rocks are pushed upward. Other mountains are made by erosion. Wind, water, or ice wears some of the land away until a mountain is left behind. **4**

This is a volcanic mountain.

The Grand Tetons are block mountains.

The Catskill Mountains were made by erosion.

4 Implicit Meaning
COMPARING AND CONTRASTING

■ The landforms in the paragraph and photographs are both alike and different. How are the landforms alike? *(They are all mountains.)* How are they different? *(They were formed in different ways.)*

UNDERSTANDING CAUSE AND EFFECT

■ Different processes cause different kinds of valleys. Most valleys are caused by erosion. What type of valley might form in an area where the land is soft? *(flat and wide river valleys)* What type of valley might form in an area where the land is hard and rocky? *(deep and thin river valleys called canyons)*

The Colorado River made the Grand Canyon.

The Mississippi River made this wide valley.

How Valleys Are Made

Like mountains, valleys can be made in different ways, too. A few of the largest valleys were made when two pieces of Earth's crust moved apart, leaving a low piece of land between them. But most valleys are made by erosion. Rivers and streams flow over the land, taking small pieces of rock and soil with them.

Over hundreds of years, erosion can make a valley. Where the land is soft, valleys are flat and wide. But where the land is hard and rocky, valleys are deep and thin. These valleys are often called canyons.

⑤

Earth's crust moved to make the Great Rift Valley.

42

Our Changing Earth

When we look at a mountain, it's hard to believe that it is slowly getting larger or smaller. But the processes that created planet Earth are still at work today. Pieces of Earth's crust are slowly sliding under our feet. Rivers are digging valleys and canyons. Weather is smoothing mountains and wearing them away. Our planet is always changing. It is our changing Earth. **6**

43

6 Implicit Meaning
IDENTIFYING MAIN IDEA

■ What is the main idea of the paragraph on this page? *(Our Earth is always changing.)*

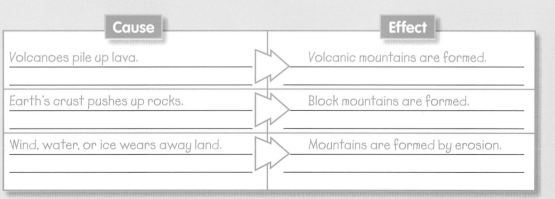

Finishing Up
MODEL IDENTIFYING CAUSE AND EFFECT

Create a cause and effect chart to guide children in reviewing causes and effects in the article

Cause	Effect
Volcanoes pile up lava.	Volcanic mountains are formed.
Earth's crust pushes up rocks.	Block mountains are formed.
Wind, water, or ice wears away land.	Mountains are formed by erosion.

Comprehension Focus
INTERPRETING PICTURES, GRAPHS, AND CHARTS

Tell children that the pictures, graphs, and charts they find in nonfiction articles can provide a great deal of information. Explain that the captions and labels can help them understand what the visual aid is all about. Tell children always to look at and read a visual aid because it often contains information that is not included in the text.

VOCABULARY

The following words appear in the article. Explain them briefly as you come to them: *system,* a group of parts that work together; *energy,* fuel that lets plants and animals move or grow; *cactus,* desert plant that needs very little water to live.

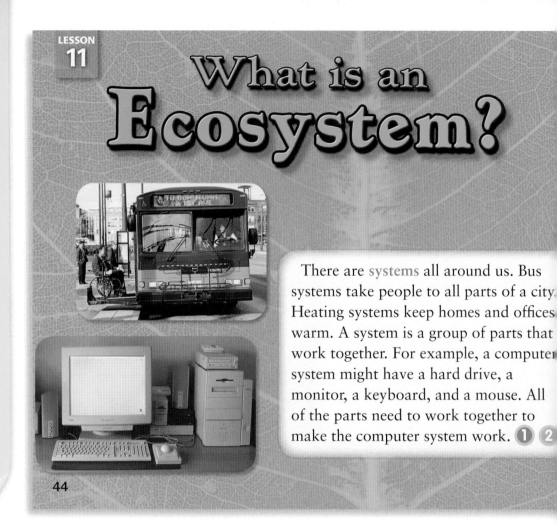

LESSON

11

What is an Ecosystem?

There are systems all around us. Bus systems take people to all parts of a city. Heating systems keep homes and offices warm. A system is a group of parts that work together. For example, a computer system might have a hard drive, a monitor, a keyboard, and a mouse. All of the parts need to work together to make the computer system work. **①** **②**

44

---

① Explicit Meaning
UNDERSTANDING DETAILS

■ Read the first sentence of this paragraph. What are some systems described on this page? *(bus system, heating system, computer system)*

② Conceptual Meaning
COMPARING AND CONTRASTING

■ Point to the two pictures on this page. How are the bus system and the computer system alike? *(The parts of each system must work together to make the system work.)*

Nature has systems, too. An ecosystem is a group of things that are found together in nature. Some of the things in an ecosystem are alive, such as animals and plants. Other things in an ecosystem are not alive, such as soil, water, light, and air. Each part of an ecosystem is important. If one part changes, other parts of the ecosystem will change, too. ❸

What are the parts of these ecosystems?

45

■ Ecosystems are nature's systems. Each part of the ecosystem must work together to make the ecosystem work. What do you think might happen if one part of an ecosystem, such as rabbits, disappeared? *(Other parts of the ecosystem might change as well. All of the animals that eat rabbits would not have enough food or would need to find a different food to eat.)*

ENGLISH LANGUAGE LEARNERS

To help children develop new vocabulary, have them point to each animal pictured on this page and repeat the name after you. Then talk about what the animal is like, including details such as its size, color, enemies, diet, and habitat. Invite children to mime the movement of these animals.

READING DIAGRAMS

- The diagram on this page can help us understand the paragraph we just read. Look at the title of this diagram. What does the diagram show? *(a food chain)*

- Why do you think the sun is shown at the top of the chain? *(Everything else must have sunlight to live.)*

- What does the mouse eat? *(seeds)*

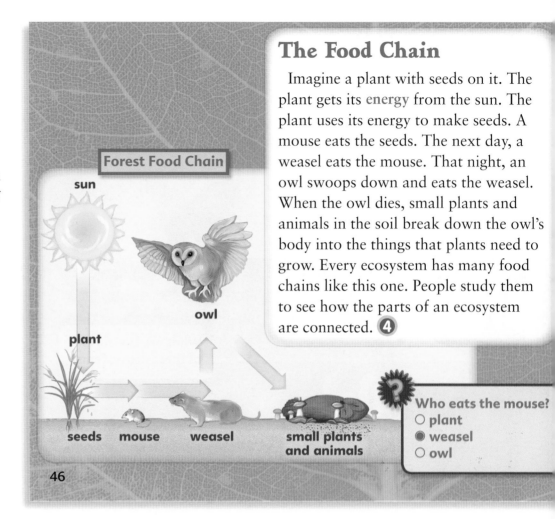

The Food Chain

Imagine a plant with seeds on it. The plant gets its **energy** from the sun. The plant uses its energy to make seeds. A mouse eats the seeds. The next day, a weasel eats the mouse. That night, an owl swoops down and eats the weasel. When the owl dies, small plants and animals in the soil break down the owl's body into the things that plants need to grow. Every ecosystem has many food chains like this one. People study them to see how the parts of an ecosystem are connected. ④

Forest Food Chain

sun

owl

plant

seeds   mouse   weasel   small plants and animals

Who eats the mouse?
- ○ plant
- ● weasel
- ○ owl

46

A World of Ecosystems

The world has many different kinds of ecosystems. Each one has different weather, plants, and animals.

The forest ecosystem has many tall trees. It gets a lot of rain or snow every year. Owls, deer, and bears are animals that live in the forest. **5**

The grassland ecosystem has more grasses than any other kind of plant. Grasslands get some rain, but not very much. Zebras, giraffes, and elephants all live in grasslands.

47

MAKING INFERENCES

■ Did you know that so many plants and animals lived in rain forests? Why is it important to protect rain forest ecosystems? *(They have more kinds of living things than any other ecosystem.)*

Rain forests are warm and rainy. Trees of all sizes grow there. Rain forests have more kinds of living things than any other ecosystem. Monkeys, parrots, and tree frogs live in rain forests. 6

Deserts can be hot or cold. But they are always very dry. Many kinds of **cactus** grow in the desert. Jackrabbits and rattlesnakes are animals that live there. 7

48

7 **Text Features**
READING MAPS

■ Point to the map of the desert. What new things can you learn by looking at the maps on this page? *(You can tell where deserts and rain forests are located.)*

Why Study Ecosystems?

People live in every ecosystem. When we change one thing in an ecosystem, many plants and animals are affected. Sometimes these changes do not cause trouble for an ecosystem. But sometimes they do. By studying how ecosystems work, we can learn how to keep our world safe and healthy. ⑧

⑧ Conceptual Meaning

IDENTIFYING CAUSE AND EFFECT

■ Why should we study how ecosystems work? *(We will know how to keep them safe and healthy.)*

Finishing Up
MODEL INTERPRETING PICTURES, GRAPHS, AND CHARTS

Create a chart to help children identify information they learned about a particular ecosystem by interpreting pictures, charts, and maps in the article.

Things in Nature	
Living Things	**Nonliving Things**
Animals For forest: mouse, weasel, owl	sun, soil, water, air.
Plants For forest: trees, plants, seeds	

Comprehension Focus
MAKING INFERENCES

Remind children that when they make inferences, they use clues from their reading and from their personal experiences. Encourage children to make inferences as they read *Save the Trees!*

VOCABULARY

The following words appear in the article. Explain them briefly as you come to them: *lumber,* wood used for building; *area,* place.

ENGLISH LANGUAGE LEARNERS

Discuss the different things that people do with trees, such as climbing them or cutting them down. Explain that trees are wood, and that people cut down trees to make things. Ask children to point to and name objects in the classroom that are made out of wood, such as furniture and pencils. Explain that builders who make things with wood call the wood lumber.

LESSON 12

Save the Trees!

Julia Hill was upset. A lumber company was cutting down too many trees. Julia wanted people to learn about this problem. She decided to climb a redwood tree that was 180 feet tall. Julia lived in the tree for the next two years. Friends brought her food and supplies. She pulled it all up with ropes. ❶

Julia's treehouse

What would it be like to live in a tree?

50

❶ **Implicit Meaning**
MAKING CONNECTIONS

■ Did you know that a person could live in a tree for two years? Try to imagine if you lived in a tree. What do you think would be hard about living in a tree for that long? *(You would not see your friends, you'd get bored, you wouldn't have TV, you would not be comfortable.)*

Some people said that Julia was strange. But she did not mind. She wanted people to care about trees. ②

The lumber company tried to chase Julia out. They cut trees around her. But Julia did not move. Instead, she was able to get on the TV news. Julia spoke about saving the trees.

Finally, the lumber company promised not to cut down trees in a certain area. At last, Julia Hill climbed down from her tree. ③

Julia Hill

Why did Julia climb down from her tree?

Redwood forest

51

② **Implicit Meaning**
MAKING INFERENCES

■ The author says that Julia did not mind that people thought she was strange. What does this show you about Julia? *(Saving the trees was very important to her.)*

③ **Implicit Meaning**
MAKING INFERENCES

■ How do you think Julia Hill felt when she came down from the tree? Why? *(She probably felt proud because she had saved the redwood trees.)*

Finishing Up
MODEL MAKING INFERENCES

Create an inference chart to help children make inferences about what Julia Hill is like as a person.

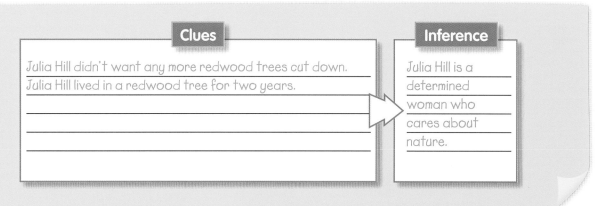

Clues	Inference
Julia Hill didn't want any more redwood trees cut down.	Julia Hill is a determined woman who cares about nature.
Julia Hill lived in a redwood tree for two years.	

Comprehension Focus
SUMMARIZING

Tell children that summarizing is a good way to check their understanding of something they read. Summarizing is retelling the most important ideas. Have children think about ideas to include in a summary as they read the article.

VOCABULARY

The following words appear in the article. Explain them briefly as you come to them: *bark*, outer layer of a tree; *rot*, to become spoiled and slowly fall apart; *cozy*, comfortable; *cases*, suitcases or boxes.

LESSON
13
What a Long, Strange Trip!

Dear Anna, ❶

We just started our trip today. Mom says that we'll visit all kinds of interesting places. She says we'll go to a forest, to a place that's covered in ice, and then to the ocean. Dad says he has some surprises, too. He says the nights will be as much fun as the days.

Your friend,

Tyra ❷

Which of the places Tyra will visit sounds most interesting to you?

52

❶ **Text Features**
PARTS OF A LETTER

■ Point to the greeting of the letter. What does it say? *(Dear Anna)* Who will get this letter? *(Anna)*

❷ **Text Features**
PARTS OF A LETTER

■ Now point to the closing of the letter. What does this part say? *(Your friend)* What does the signature say? *(Tyra)* This is the name of the person who wrote the letter. It looks like this whole story is made up of letters from Tyra to Anna.

Dear Anna,

Dad really surprised us last night. We stayed in a treehouse hotel! The rooms were small. But they had lights, heat, and a bathroom.

We met the man who built the treehouse. He told us that treehouses need to be built in strong trees. He also said that it was important not to scrape the bark. If the bark is harmed, bugs and water can get inside the tree. Then the tree might rot. ③

Sleeping in a treehouse was fun. When the wind blew, we felt the treehouse sway from side to side.

Your friend,

Tyra

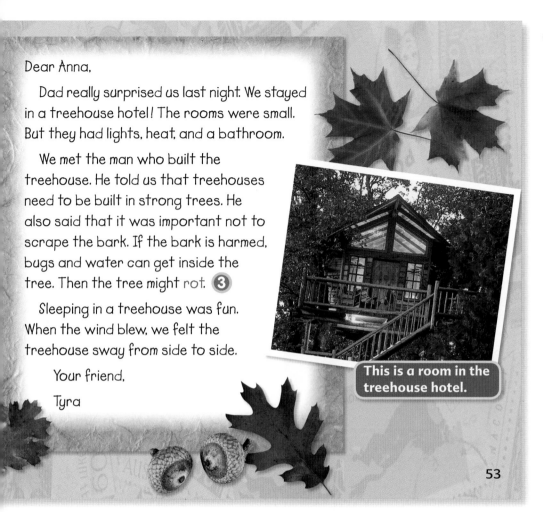

This is a room in the treehouse hotel.

53

③ **Implicit Meaning**
MAKING INFERENCES

■ The treehouse that Tyra stayed in was a whole building up in the branches of a tree. Why do you think treehouses need to be built in strong trees? *(So that the treehouse won't fall or harm the tree.)*

MAKING CONNECTIONS

■ Tyra has been to a hotel in a tree and a hotel made out of ice. Which type of hotel would you rather stay in?

ENGLISH LANGUAGE LEARNERS

To help children learn the meanings of words such as *freezing* and *cozy*, display an ice cube and a blanket or sweater. Wrap yourself up in the blanket and say a sentence that tells how you feel, "This blanket makes me feel nice and cozy." Hold out the ice cube and say, "This ice is freezing! My hand is very cold." Invite volunteers to act out sentences using the words *cozy* and *freezing*.

Dear Anna,

We are in a hotel that is really COOL! The whole building is made of ice and snow. Even the chairs are made of ice. It is freezing inside! I wear my coat during the day. But at night, we are warm and cozy. Thick, heavy sleeping bags cover the beds. ④

A hotel worker said the building would melt this spring. She said the owners would build a whole new hotel next winter! ⑤

Your friend,

Tyra

This is a room in the ice hotel.

54

⑤ Implicit Meaning
IDENTIFYING CAUSE AND EFFECT

■ Why do you think the ice hotel gets rebuilt every year? *(In the spring the temperature gets warm and the building melts. Then when the weather is cold again, they can rebuild the hotel.)*

Dear Anna,

Today we flew to Florida. After our stay in an ice hotel, we were ready for the warm beach. Once again, Dad had a surprise. We are staying in an underwater hotel! **6**

We checked in on land. Then we put on diving suits. We put our dry clothes in special cases. Then we swam to our room! Our room is like any hotel room. The best part is the huge window. I can watch the fish swim by!

We will be home soon and I'm ready. We have stayed in some strange places. But I still like my home the best!

Your friend,

Tyra

This is a room in the underwater hotel.

In what order did Tyra visit these places?

_2_ ice hotel

_3_ underwater hotel

_1_ treehouse hotel

55

6 Implicit Meaning
MAKING INFERENCES

■ Tyra says that after visiting the ice hotel, her family flew to Florida. What does this tell you about the distance between the ice hotel and Florida? What other story clues help you decide? *(The ice hotel was probably far from Florida. It was far enough to fly by plane. Also, one place was cold and icy and the other had a warm beach.)*

Finishing Up
MODEL SUMMARIZING

Create a Summary Web to help children summarize the story.

My Summmary is About

different hotels Tyra visited

Important Points

Tyra learned that treehouses are built in strong trees.
Tyra stayed in a cold ice hotel.
Tyra's family stayed in an underwater hotel where they swam to their room.

Summary

Tyra's family visited some very unusual places: a treehouse hotel, an ice hotel, and an underwater hotel.

Comprehension Focus
ASKING AND
ANSWERING QUESTIONS

Tell children that when they read an article, they can learn a lot by asking questions about things they want to know or things they don't understand. Then they can look for answers to those questions as they read. Suggest that they think of questions they have about climate and look for answers as they read this article.

VOCABULARY

The following words appear in the article. Explain them briefly as you come to them: *usually,* most often; *tropical,* related to places near the equator; *polar;* related to places near the North and South Poles; *temperate,* related to places between the poles and the equator.

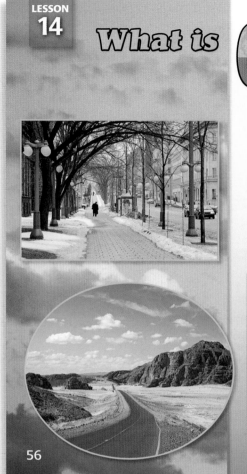

LESSON
14 What is Climate?

A climate is the kind of weather a place has most of the time. In a hot climate, the weather is often hot. In a cold climate, the weather is often cold. Places where the weather changes a lot have a climate, too. Their climate tells what the weather is usually like at each time of year. ❶

56

❶ **Text Feature**
PICTURES

■ These pictures show different climates. Which one looks most like the place where we live?

■ Would you say our climate is hot, cold, or something different?

The earth has different climates because of the sun. At the middle of the earth, near the equator, the sunshine is very strong. This strong sunshine makes the equator very hot. The sunshine near the North and the South Poles is weaker, so those climates are much colder. ❷

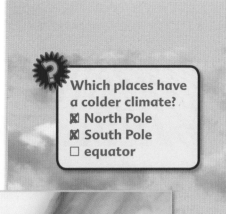

Which places have a colder climate?
☒ **North Pole**
☒ **South Pole**
☐ **equator**

equator

sun

Sunshine is stronger near the earth's equator.

57

❷ **Explicit Meaning**

UNDERSTANDING MAIN IDEA AND DETAILS

■ Different areas of Earth have different climates because of the sun. Why is the equator hot? *(The sunshine is very strong there.)* Why are the North and South Poles cold? *(The sunshine is weaker there.)*

❸ Explicit Meaning
UNDERSTANDING MAIN IDEA AND DETAILS

- What are the names of the three climates on Earth? *(tropical, polar, temperate)*
- Which climate is the hottest? *(tropical)*
- Which climate is the coldest? *(polar)*

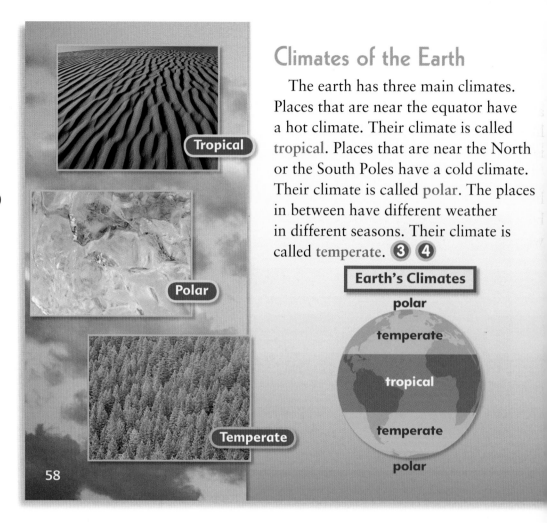

Tropical

Polar

Temperate

58

Climates of the Earth

The earth has three main climates. Places that are near the equator have a hot climate. Their climate is called tropical. Places that are near the North or the South Poles have a cold climate. Their climate is called polar. The places in between have different weather in different seasons. Their climate is called temperate. ❸ ❹

Earth's Climates

polar

temperate

tropical

temperate

polar

❹ Text Features
READING DIAGRAMS

- This diagram can help us to see where the different climates are. Look at the diagram. Using what you know about climates, can you see which part of the earth has the warmest climate? *(the center of Earth)* Which parts of the earth have the coldest climates? *(the very top and bottom parts)*

The Tropical Climate

Can you imagine a place that's hot day and night, all year long? That's what it's like in the tropical climate. This climate is near the earth's equator. **5**

About half of the world's people live in a tropical climate. Maybe that's because they would rather live where the weather is sunny and warm.

Tropical Climate

Equator

Tropical climates have warm weather.

59

5 Implicit Meaning
MAKING INFERENCES

- How would you probably dress in a tropical climate? *(in light clothes or maybe a bathing suit)*

- How does the photo on this page help you decide? *(It shows a place you might go swimming.)*

ENGLISH LANGUAGE LEARNERS

To help children recognize the terms equator, North Pole, and South Pole, display a globe and locate the places. Have children point to each place and repeat the name after you. Identify which places are hot and which are cold. Then locate regions of the earth that have temperate climates. Say the name of each place and have children repeat after you.

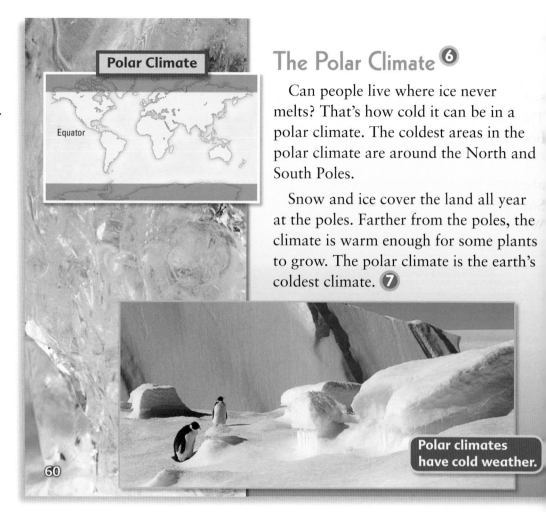

Polar Climate

Equator

60

Polar climates have cold weather.

The Polar Climate **6**

Can people live where ice never melts? That's how cold it can be in a polar climate. The coldest areas in the polar climate are around the North and South Poles.

Snow and ice cover the land all year at the poles. Farther from the poles, the climate is warm enough for some plants to grow. The polar climate is the earth's coldest climate. **7**

The Temperate Climate

What is the only climate with four seasons? It is the temperate climate. The word temperate means "not too hot or too cold."

Places with a temperate climate don't always have nice weather, though. Summer weather can be very hot. Winter weather can drop below freezing. **8**

The seasons change in temperate climates.

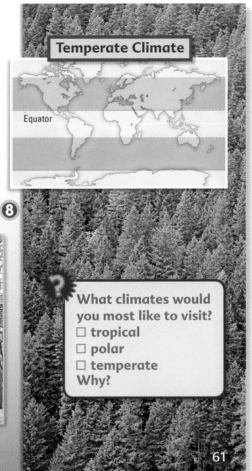

Temperate Climate

Equator

What climates would you most like to visit?
☐ **tropical**
☐ **polar**
☐ **temperate**
Why?

61

8 **Text Features**
READING MAPS

■ Can you find the United States on the world map? Which climate zone does it mostly lie in? *(temperate)*

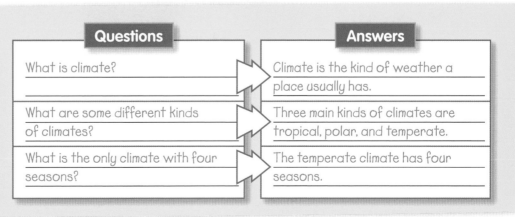

Finishing Up
MODEL ASKING AND ANSWERING QUESTIONS

Guide children in listing questions on an asking and answering chart to apply the strategy to the article.

Questions	Answers
What is climate?	Climate is the kind of weather a place usually has.
What are some different kinds of climates?	Three main kinds of climates are tropical, polar, and temperate.
What is the only climate with four seasons?	The temperate climate has four seasons.

Comprehension Focus
MAKING CONNECTIONS

Tell children that when they link new information to something they already know they are making connections. Some ways of making connections are thinking of related things they have done, have read about, or have heard about. Ask them to try to make connections like these as they read *Arctic Life*.

VOCABULARY

The following words appear in the article. Explain them briefly as you come to them: *hooves,* the feet of certain animals like cows or deer; *modern,* not old fashioned; *harsh,* cruel or rough.

LESSON 15

Arctic Life

Polar bears live in the Arctic.

The Arctic

Do you know any places that are very cold? One cold place has lots of snow and ice. It is the home of polar bears, reindeer, and walruses. The North Pole is there, too. What is this part of the world? It's the Arctic! **1**

62

1 Implicit Meaning
MAKING CONNECTIONS

■ What are some places you know about that are very cold?

Many kinds of animals live in the Arctic. Arctic foxes and Arctic hares live on land. These animals have white fur in winter. Their thick fur keeps them warm. Reindeer also live in the Arctic. Their large hooves help them walk on snow. ❷

Arctic hares have white fur in winter.

Walruses need a thick layer of fat to stay warm in the icy water.

Seals and walruses swim in the Arctic Ocean. Sometimes they climb onto the land or ice. A thick layer of fat keeps these animals warm. The fat is called blubber. ❸

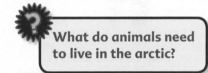

What do animals need to live in the arctic?

63

❷ Implicit Meaning
MAKING CONNECTIONS

- Did you ever see a pair of snow-shoes or skis? How are the rein-deer's hooves like snowshoes? *(Their hooves help them walk on snow, just as snowshoes do.)*

ENGLISH LANGUAGE LEARNERS

Display a globe or map and locate the Arctic for children. Then ask children to point to the Arctic and say its name. Explain that the Arctic is very cold. Ask the children about their experiences with cold. Have they ever been to a cold place? Have they ever put their hand in the freezer or held a piece of ice? Help them to relate these experiences to their understanding of the Arctic.

❸ Conceptual Meaning
ANIMAL CHARACTERISTICS

- There are many different kinds of animals that live in the arctic. What are some ways that they stay warm? *(They have fur or blubber.)*

4 Explicit Meaning

IDENTIFYING MAIN IDEA AND DETAILS

- What is the main idea of this page? *(People live in the Arctic.)*

- Name two groups of people who live in the Arctic. *(Inuit and Sami)*

People live in the Arctic, too. The Inuit are one group of Arctic people. Most Inuit live in houses. They shop in stores for clothes and food. But some Inuit still hunt for food. They build igloos when they go on a long hunt.

Inuit children

Some Sami still raise herds of reindeer.

64

The Sami are another group of Arctic people. Many Sami live in modern towns. But some Sami travel all the time. These Sami own herds of reindeer. The reindeer must keep moving to find food. The Sami must travel with their reindeer. **4 5**

5 Implicit Meaning

COMPARING AND CONTRASTING

- How are the Inuit and Sami people alike? How are they different? *(Alike: Most Inuit and some Sami people live in modern homes or towns. Different: Only the Sami keep herds of reindeer.)*

Winter in the Arctic is very **harsh**. Snow covers all the land. Ice covers the Arctic Ocean. It gets so cold that a person's breath freezes! In some places the sun never rises. The sky is dark all day and all night.

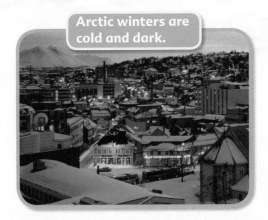

Arctic winters are cold and dark.

In summer, some parts of the Arctic stay snowy. But in other parts the snow melts. Plants grow, and flowers bloom. In some places the sun never sets. The sky is bright all day and night. ❻

The Arctic is a home for many different animals, plants, and people.

Arctic summers are sunny and bright.

65

❻ **Explicit Meaning**
IDENTIFYING MAIN IDEA AND DETAILS

■ How are winters in the Arctic harsh? (*Snow covers all the land. Ice covers the Arctic Ocean. It gets very cold. In some places the sun never rises. The sky is dark all day and night.*)

■ What happens in some parts of the Arctic during the summer? (*snow melts, plants grow, flowers bloom, birds are born*)

Finishing Up
MODEL MAKING CONNECTIONS

Create a chart to record the connections children make with information in the article.

Making Connections

What I already know	What I learned	Connections I made
The Arctic is very cold.	Many kinds of animals live in the Arctic.	Some animals have blubber or fur to stay warm in the cold weather.

Comprehension Focus
DISTINGUISHING FANTASY AND REALITY

Tell children that some stories they read may contain events that could not happen in real life. These stories are called fantasies. Fantasy stories may also include things that could happen in real life. Have children note things that are real and things that could not really happen as they read.

VOCABULARY

The following words appear in the article. They can be explained briefly as you come to them: *narrow,* not wide; *wrapped,* curled around, covering; *vanished,* disappeared.

LESSON
16

RAIN FOREST ADVENTURE

Adam had gone to the zoo with his parents and his little sister, Jess. Their favorite part was the rain forest area. It had many interesting animals.

"I loved the snakes," said Jess.

"The monkeys were the best," said Adam. "I think I'll name my new toy monkey Jake." Mom and Dad smiled. It had been a great day. ❷

66

❶ **Text Features**
PUNCTUATION

- In this sentence a character is talking. Look at the marks before the word *I* and after the word *snakes*. What do we call these marks? *(quotation marks)*

- What do they show you? *(They show a speaker's exact words.)*

❷ **Explicit Meaning**
UNDERSTANDING DETAILS

- What were Adam's favorite animals at the zoo? *(the monkeys)*

When they got home, Dad said, "Off to bed, Adam. And you too, Jake."

Adam put Jake on his dresser and got into bed.

"I'm glad I got you. You're my rain forest friend," Adam said to Jake. Then Adam yawned and fell fast asleep.

Soon Adam began to dream that he was in a rain forest. The rain forest felt hot and sticky. Tall trees with huge leaves were growing everywhere. Birds were singing above him. Adam saw a narrow path. He began to walk down it. ③

67

③ Conceptual Meaning

DISTINGUISHING FANTASY AND REALITY

■ Could Adam be in the rain forest in real life? How do you know? *(No, he couldn't be in the rain forest. I can tell because he just went to bed and he would have to travel a long way to get to the rain forest.)*

MAKING PREDICTIONS

■ A lot is happening to Adam since he fell asleep. What would you do if you were Adam and these things were really happening? What do you think will happen next? (*I would run away as fast as I could. That's what Adam will do.*)

Find these anim
in the picture:
monkey
snake
jaguar

The path led Adam deep into the rain forest. It was almost dark. The tree branches looked like fingers that were long and curled.

Adam heard a hissing sound over his head. He looked up. It was a snake, wrapped around a branch! ④

Adam ran down the path before the snake could move. Then he heard a roar behind him. Was it a jaguar?

68

Suddenly, the leaves above Adam moved. He jumped right off the path. He looked up to see Jake!

Jake said, "Don't be afraid, I'm here to help you."

Adam said, "I think I'm lost. Can you help me find my way out of here?" Jake took Adam's hand and started to lead him out of the rain forest. ⑤

Is Jake a real rain forest monkey?

no

How can you tell?

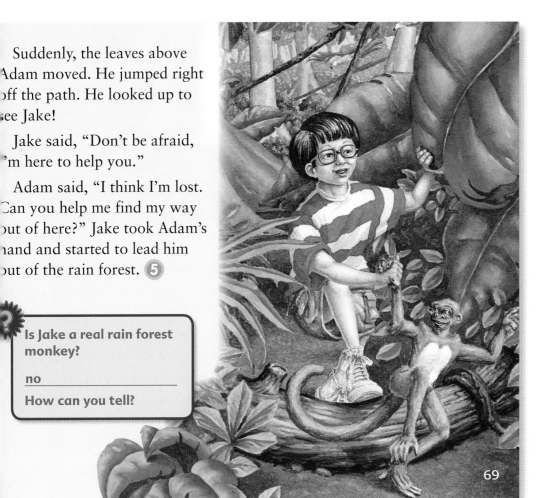

69

⑤ Conceptual Meaning
DISTINGUISHING FANTASY AND REALITY

■ What happens in Adam's dream that could never happen in real life? *(Adam's toy monkey walks and helps lead him out of the rain forest.)*

MAKING PREDICTIONS

■ What do you think made the loud crash? *(Maybe something fell.)*

Adam followed closely behind Jake. They tiptoed right past a sleeping jaguar. They walked below some singing birds. Then they sneaked under a huge snake wrapped around a branch.

Suddenly it started to rain. The path became muddy and slippery. Adam and Jake could barely see where they were going. Then there was a loud crash. Adam jumped! **6**

70

Adam woke up with a start. He wasn't in the rain forest. He was in his own bed! He looked out the window. It was raining hard outside. A tree branch was crashing against the house. **7**

Adam sat up and saw that Jake had **vanished** from the dresser. He felt something in his bed. He looked down. There was Jake, right beside him!

71

7 Implicit Meaning
IDENTIFYING CAUSE AND EFFECT

■ What made the crashing noise in real life? *(a tree branch outside Adam's bedroom window)*

ENGLISH LANGUAGE LEARNERS

Point out the idiom "woke up with a start." Explain that this means to wake up suddenly with surprise. Ask children to share experiences they have had waking up suddenly from a dream. Then have children act out what Adam looked like when he woke up.

Finishing Up
MODEL DISTINGUISHING FANTASY AND REALITY

Create a chart to record realistic and fantastic details from the story.

Could Really Happen	Could Not Really Happen
A boy could visit the zoo.	A real monkey could not talk.
A boy could get a toy monkey.	A toy monkey could not rescue a boy.
A boy could have a dream about a rain forest.	

Glossary

A

area   An area is a certain place.

attacks   When something attacks, it tries to hurt someone or something.

B

bands   Bands are stripes that go around something.

brag   To brag is to speak too highly about yourself.

C

cactus   A cactus is a thick plant that doesn't have leaves or need much water to live.

cases   Cases are boxes or containers.

cozy   Cozy means warm and comfortable.

D

danger   A person or animal that is in danger may be harmed or killed.

darts   When something darts, it moves quickly and suddenly.

decorate   To decorate something is to add things to it to make it look good.

discovered   Something that has been discovered has been found.

E

echo   An echo is a sound bouncing off of something hard.

embarrassed   To be embarrassed means to be shy or ashamed about something you have done.

energy   Energy is power that can be used to do or make things.

erosion   Erosion is the slow wearing away of rock or soil by water or by the weather.

erupts   When something erupts, it bursts out suddenly.

exist   To exist is to live or be real.

fossils   Fossils are the remains of animals or plants that lived long ago.

harsh   Harsh means very unpleasant or harmful.

hibernate   To hibernate means to spend the winter in a deep sleep.

hooves   The hooves of an animal are the hard lower part of its feet.

interesting   Something that is interesting is something you want to know more about.

landforms   Landforms are natural features of the surface of the earth, such as mountains and hills.

lumber   Lumber is big pieces of wood cut from trees.

magma   Magma is melted rock that is found deep in the earth.

mammals   Mammals are animals that usually have hair or fur and have live babies.

modern   Modern means new and up to date.

narrow   Something narrow is not very wide in comparison to its length.

poison   Poison is something harmful to touch or taste.

polar   Polar means near the North or South Poles.

pollen   Pollen is a powder made by plants.

prey   Prey is an animal hunted by another animal for food.

processes   Processes are sets of things that happen or are done in a certain order.

prove   To prove something is to show that it is a fact.

 R

reporters   Reporters are people who tell the news.

rot   To rot means to become spoiled and slowly fall apart.

 S

skull   The bones that make up the head are the skull.

systems   Systems are sets of things that work together.

 T

temperate   A temperate place rarely gets very hot or very cold.

tide   The tide is the force that brings water to and from the shore.

tiny   Tiny means very small.

tropical   A tropical place is usually hot and damp.

 V

vanished   Vanished means to have disappeared suddenly.

 W

warning   A warning tells people or animals that there might be danger.

webbed   Webbed feet have skin between the toes.

wrapped   Wrapped means to be placed tightly around something.

Teacher Notes

Teacher Notes